Breaking Through Chaos

A Guide to Help You Bring Balance Back to Life

Liza Davis

This book is dedicated to my grandparents, John and Margaret Elizabeth Copeland. It is also dedicated to the entrepreneur's entrepreneur, Julius C. "Bud" Shaw.

CONTENTS

Maintaining You and Functioning Effectively

ACKNOWLEDGMENTS

This project has been so rewarding for me. I count it a blessing to be able to share with you the lessons I've learned on my journey that work when you work them. My prayer is that the work will inspire you to grow and live your life in a way that is more authentic and satisfying. It is also my great pleasure to thank those who have helped make this book a physical reality.

To my team, there is truly power in numbers. I could not count this book as an accomplishment without your expertise and due diligence. Your belief in my vision means everything.

To Gina Devee and my fellow Divine Living Queens, you ladies rock! Thank you for the high vibe environment.

To my family, Brenda Davis, Jason Davis, Helen Gordon, and Vaughn Waters, thank you for your unconditional love and support and for being such a great help to me during this process.

To Valorie Burton, thank you for opening my eyes to see the porch and thank you Alicia Booker for helping me to get off of it.

To Cynthia Craig, Sherita Cherry, Lescia Mescudi, Taheerah Norman, Tip White, Annette Gardner Johnson, and Georgia Wolfe Samuels, thank you for helping me to get my "entire" life back. Your example has silently ministered to me on so many levels.

To Kim Smith, I cannot thank you enough. You have given of yourself in so many ways, and I am grateful for your unconditional love and friendship.

To Robert Wright, I wish I could take my heart out and put it inside you so you could feel what I feel when I think of you. Your love and friendship to me are priceless, and I am so thankful for you holding my hand and walking this journey with me. I absolutely could not ask for a better friend. To Sidney Wright, God knew what He was doing when He brought you into my life. You are restoration at its finest. I love you.

INTRODUCTION

In 2011, I moved to Destin, Florida. It was beautiful. I moved into a gorgeous condo on a private beach. We had amazing sunsets, two-hour breakfast, and Pilates on the beach in the mornings. It was a beautiful place to unwind and relax. Destin was a huge difference from Atlanta; everything was at a much slower pace. At that time in my life, I needed it. For the previous three years, I had been working over 100 plus hours a week, I was exhausted. So I welcomed this opportunity to slow it down a bit. I had decided to take a year off from work and Destin just seemed like the best place to do it.

In the evenings, I would take time out to sit on the beach, watch the sunset, and reflect on life. I was grateful to see the unlimited beauty of the sun and the water and the sand. It was very peaceful. Many times I found myself just thanking God that this girl who grew up in the projects of Buffalo, New York, even had the means to enjoy this space for a while. During one of my prayer and meditation moments, I found myself crying uncontrollably. It felt as if the moment and space I was in, was my permission slip to acknowledge really how I was feeling. For years, I kept myself so busy, too busy to sit and acknowledge where I was in my life, how I felt about it and address it. Even though geography had me in this lovely place, on the inside, I didn't feel so lovely. The truth was I was tired, depressed, and unfulfilled.

Taking yourself out of familiar territory can either show you how well you have it or where you are lacking. For me it was the later. I had not been living at all; I had been existing. There is a huge difference. I was very good at my job, but it had only scratched the surface of my gifts and talents. It didn't challenge me; it didn't help me to grow to the heights I knew I could. I stayed with it out of comfort and the fear of challenges that come with digging deeper. I had always wanted a family, but I had been a participant and witness to so many unsuccessful relationships, that it was just easier to stay single. My mother would tell me that I had never met a stranger; everyone was my friend. The reality is everyone is not your friend, and the disappointment that came with the lessons associated with that truth made me feel like something was wrong with me. There was a whole lot in my life I had continuously swept under the rug and then trampled on with my busyness believing the harder and faster I stomped, they would disappear under the carpet.

Thank God that He never leaves us, He is the best counselor. He knows all and sees all and can open up truth to you when you have brainwashed yourself into believing something that isn't true for you. That moment on the beach was my stop sign. It showed me that although everything seemed so right, on the inside there was something very wrong. Chaos is defined as complete disorder and confusion, and confusion is what my life was experiencing. The truth was that my physical life did not exemplify what I wanted for my life from the perspective of my heart. They were out of alignment, the balance was lost, thus came the tears and the broken heart. It helped me to see that we can cover up pain from unfulfilled dreams and desires, but that will not make it go away, it is only a cover up. Disappointment can still reveal itself through tears, frowns, and wrinkled foreheads. My prayer is for Breaking Through Chaos to help you do just that, break through the chaos and bring the balance back to your life and leave you renewed and fulfilled.

Liza

HOW TO USE THIS BOOK

In this book, I have included some of the most important lessons I have learned on my journey to bringing back the balance. These are lessons that I still carry with me to this day. They brought me from negative in my pocket to six figures, from low self-esteem to confidence and courage that I could beat any giant (just hand me a slingshot), and from a dessert to an overflowing spring of love and positive energy.

I read several books at one time. What I have come to learn is if you take a book in bite-size pieces and allow yourself the space to chew (break it down) and savor (get the lesson) what you are reading, that book will have a greater impact on you, than going through it in a week. Everything should have a place and purpose in your life, right down to the very penny in your pocket. My prayer is that you will allow this book to have a purpose in your life and do what it says it can do, bring back the balance.

I do not embellish a lot; this book is just straight to the point. My suggestion is to find yourself where you can in the pages, in sort of a get in where you fit in type of way, and put an action to the lesson you learn. Use the journal questions to write out your thoughts and feelings about the lessons. This is a great way to notate your growth. Lastly, I find it very beneficial to turn your lesson into a positive affirmation for yourself that you can meditate on in your prayer and meditation time. You will find this very helpful in creating positive emotion. So grab a pen and let's get started.

PUTTING FIRST THINGS FIRST

I love the story of the Proverbs 31 woman. I believe she is a superhero to Christian women. I cannot remember one women's conference I've attended where she is not mentioned. She has it all together, thriving in business, her family and community look up to her as a sign of strength, and she has a solid spiritual foundation. I have read the story numerous times. All of the scriptures concerning the Proverbs 31 woman give hope, encouragement, and life. There is one scripture that in my opinion is the foundation for any level of success we strive to achieve in our lives, Proverbs 31:17. I believe it is explained best in the amplified bible.

> Proverbs 31:17 AMP She equips herself with strength (spiritual, mental, and physical fitness for her God-given task) And makes her arms strong.

Take note of the order of the explanation of the word strength. The scripture explains it as spiritual, mental, and physical fitness for her God-given task. It does not say physical, spiritual, mental or even mental, physical, spiritual. It begins with the spiritual aspect because we are spirit beings. We are a spirit, we possess a soul, our mind, will, and emotions, and we live in a physical body. Thus the spiritual, mental, physical order.

Let us consider a person attempting to lose weight without success or temporary success. They are working out and eating differently. So why are they not seeing results or experience results that are not lasting? There can be many reason as to why they are not successful. For this example, let us consider the person is an emotional eater. This problem would need to be addressed in the soul because the mind, will, and emotional state of the person is what is creating the problem.

Setting this order for balance as a standard for yourself will begin to clear up just about any issue you may be experiencing almost immediately. Mostly because your view of the situation will change, you will begin to see things not just with your physical eyes, but with your spiritual eyes as well.

JOURNAL QUESTIONS:

What problems are you experiencing where despite your efforts, you are not seeing the lasting results you desire?

Do your beliefs in this area of your life encourage you to be your best self?

Does your environment, be it through relationships or otherwise, encourage the results you are expecting?

What is the one action you can do today to change the situation?

UNAPOLOGETIC AUTHENTICITY

GETTING CLEAR ABOUT HOW YOU DESIRE TO LIVE YOUR LIFE

There are two ways you can live your life. You can choose to live the way that makes other people happy or the way that makes you happy and inspires others. Here is the open book answer, choose you. Going back to our foundation of the true order of balance, when we decide to do things that take us away from our natural desires, the struggle begins. When your reasons for why you do what you do differ from what is in your heart to do, the battle begins. Our physical lives are a direct reflection of what we believe and how we think. We know that with the struggle, a lack of fulfillment is not far behind. Other people looking at our lives and not seeing the success that comes with decisions made from the heart will begin to question your decisions and your path in this life God gave YOU responsibility for. Although it can be very hard to stomach criticisms from someone else about your choices, understand that you have opened the door for it when you made the decision not to operate from a place of truth for yourself. When we operate from someone else's truth we open the door for their say so and opinions in our lives. When you live your life from your truth, when the questions and personal judgments come, your responses will educate, inspire, and empower a person with a clear understanding as to your way of living. We have the power to change the reflection of our lives.

Answers and empowerment that come from a place of personal truth will always be respected even if they are not accepted as another's way of living. You will not accept anything less. As you begin to be clear about your life and choices and decisions, your conversation around them will solely be to enlighten and empower another. Living your life from a place of authenticity is freeing and very attractive, but it requires you getting honest with yourself. Once you do, you will no longer feel the need to explain your why, but live because of it.

JOURNAL QUESTIONS:

Are there areas in your life where you seek permission or acceptance from others to live out your desires and why?

A PECULIAR PEOPLE

ALLOWING INDIVIDUALITY TO BE A BLESSING

The one thing I love about authenticity is how it uses our individuality to bless and empower one another. Can you imagine if we were all the same? Life would be so boring. I love meeting people and hearing their stories and their successes. Considering we don't all take the same path, there is plenty of opportunity for growth in listening to someone else's way of doing things. Our individuality sets us apart from one another. To be peculiar is to be set apart. Embrace the times when your differences from another are acknowledged. These are opportunities you can use as exercises to help you become more comfortable with your individuality. Everyone is not going to agree with how you do things. Everyone will not celebrate all of your choices. When you are comfortable with the discomfort that can and will come at times from you being you, is when you have truly owned your authenticity. How can anyone else appreciate it, if you do not. Be mindful in these moments to not compare yourself to others, it is not healthy. We are all called to do different things, even if they are similar in nature. Move forward with the confidence that you and your path are unique. What you are doing is enough for you and what you are called to do.

JOURNAL QUESTIONS:

Do your relationships inspire you to be better or keep you comfortable where you are?

Is there any part of your individuality that you are afraid to share with others or anything that hinders your ability to share your true self?

What are some ways you can share your individuality more?

THE PEANUT GALLERY

NOT BEING MOVED BY OPINION

Try not to measure your level of success by a number of cheers you receive from the crowd. Just because someone is not cheering does not mean they are not impacted by you in a positive way. Everyone handles heart surgery differently. You do not need to justify the decisions you own to anyone. The results that come from them will answer any questions. Stand firm on what you believe. Do not allow the fears of others to dictate your next move. Just because they believe something will not work or happen for them does not make it truth for you. You cannot live a life where fulfillment is dependent on another's interpretation of your success. We have to be able to celebrate even if we are the only one in attendance at the party.

JOURNAL QUESTIONS:

How do the opinions of others influence your decisions?

Are you comfortable with making choices about your life that others may disagree with? If not, why?

ALLOWING CHARACTER TO UPLEVEL YOUR LIFE

TAKING YOUR YOUR LIFE FROM MEDIOCRITY TO EXCELLENCE

Sometimes we will find ourselves so focused on the big things that we ignore those hidden gems that produce the big things. We may look at the bigger house, the nice shiny car, and the huge international business as the things that uplevel our lives. These things come as a result of the uplevel. The uplevel comes as a result of your character and character my friend, is different for everyone. Although we all have "excellence" DNA because God created us in His excellence, we have to believe and receive this truth for ourselves. When we begin to own this truth, we will set the bar for our character development to the excellence standard. This in no way means perfect, but it does mean that you strive to do your best. Excellence is lacking on so many areas in our society. We've gotten so comfortable with doing the bare minimum, just enough to get by. Doing the bare minimum will keep you in a state of mediocrity because you are not doing anything to elevate yourself or a situation. If we want better, we must do better. Although character can be found in the simple things of life, it can require us to dig deep. Many of the choices we make come from habit and sometimes breaking these habits requires us to deal with some major heart issues we've been avoiding. Character development takes you from what is comfortable to what is necessary to live life your best life.

JOURNAL QUESTIONS:

What areas in your life do you not strive to do your best and why?

Do you feel your life is worth more than what you put into it everyday? If yes, what are some ways you can begin to raise the bar with your character?

THE COMMON DENOMINATOR

A CENTERED LIFE

We are the common denominator in every area of our lives, our business, our families, our finances, our health. At the end of the day when we want to blame everyone and everything for what is going wrong or even give credit for everything going right, we have to look at ourselves. It is our choices and decisions that we have made that have put us where we are. Ultimately it will be our choices and decisions that will take us where we desire to go. How we operate in one area will determine how we operate in another. Although challenges come in different forms, the person making the decisions in them is the same. Which is why it makes so much sense to begin with self when we want to make adjustments in different areas. We can change the furniture, the makeup, the clothes, even the job, but if the woman making the changes is not happy, those changes will not make her happy. Changes are lasting when a woman makes them as a result of internal desire for something different. We make the water hot or cold. All the more reason why it is so important for us to keep ourselves centered on those things that keep us in a state of peace and joy, and nurture and protect that space.

JOURNAL QUESTIONS:

What are some practices you have in place to maintain your peace and keep you centered on those beliefs that are important to you? Are they working for you?

Do you find yourself blaming undesirable situations in your life on others and or situations? If so, what are some ways you can begin to take your power back in these situations?

OBEDIENCE VS. RESPONSIBILITY

PRACTICAL MATURITY

Obedience is doing what you are told to do. Being responsible is doing what you need to do without being told. There is a big difference. We cannot expect mature manifestations while we are operating with a child like mentality. The owner of the business does not stop doing business today because they are not "feeling it" today. If you tell a young boy to go and cut the grass and then leave him alone to do it, nine times out of ten he will leave to do something else as well. Children are not fully developed. They are easily distracted and have not fully grasped the importance of being consistent and completing a thing. When they have grown in those areas, they will have truly learned the importance of responsibility. Likewise, if there are areas where you find yourself easily distracted or need reminding of what needs to be done, know that this is probably why you do not see the manifestation you desire. It may be time to get honest with yourself about how your true character is affecting your reality. To whom much is given, much is required. If the role you are seeking to play hasn't manifested yet, take a moment to examine the steps you've taken. Are you operating with the discipline that is required to operate in that role successfully? Dr. Wayne Dyer said it best; "you attract what you are, not what you want."

JOURNAL QUESTIONS:

Where do you find yourself distracted or lacking consistency in your life?

Are you doing everything you know to do to achieve the results you desire in your life? Do you know everything that needs to be done to have what you want, have you done your due diligence in researching what your desires require?

1

---

[1] Dr. Wayne M. Dyer, *The Power of Intention* (Hay House, 2005)

ENERGY BEGETS ENERGY AND SUCCESS BEGETS SUCCESS

HOW INFLUENCE CAN PROMOTE GROWTH AND TRANSFORMATION

Have you ever known anyone who constantly surrounds themselves with doubt and unbelief to be super successful? Neither have I. I am a firm believer in the saying, "birds of a feather, flock together." Everything about you may not be the same, but deep down there are some very similar foundational issues that keep you connected to one another. Now may be a good time to re-examine the company you keep. *Jim Rohn said it best, "You are the average of the five people you spend the most time with." We rub off on one another. Hanging with broke people will keep you broke, and I mean that spiritually, mentally, and physically. Surrounding yourself with people who know more than you will keep you in a state of learning and growing. The people you keep around you matter.

JOURNAL QUESTIONS:

Do you spend a considerable amount of time with people who do not serve your purpose well?

If yes, why and what is stopping you from having that necessary conversation?

[2]

---

[2] Kai Sato "Why The People Around You Are Crucial to Your Success," www.entrepreneur.com/233444

LIVING HIGH VIBE

USING ENERGY FOR MANIFESTATION

Is life as you live it giving off a high vibration where you experience fulfillment and excitement from your decisions? Or is it low vibration where you feel like you are just existing from day to day? The energy from others we surround ourselves with and the choices we make are all contributing factors. Become sensitive to your life's vibration. Doing so can change life for you as you know it. The energy of your life should inspire you to greatness and impact others as well. High vibration can come from the little things you do as far as where you shop or what you eat. It can also come from the bigger things such as what you read and places you travel to. Living High vibe is having a high frequency of life. It is exhilarating, it thrills you with excitement, and encourages you to get those things done you desire to do. As you begin to see your desires manifest in your life, the more wind you will get beneath your wings. When we are soaring we kill the doubt, we kill the procrastination, we kill the buzzard mentality.

JOURNAL QUESTIONS:

What are some of the things you to do that create excitement in your life and why are they so enjoyable to you?

Think back to some of your greatest accomplishments and reflect on your energy level at that time. How can you create that same level of energy for things you are looking to accomplish?

CHALLENGE: THE EXERCISE OF CHAMPIONS

LIVING IN THE AFFIRMATIVE

Living in the affirmative is all about the yes and amen and your ability to receive it. You are created with ever increasing life. A life that is increasing is living in the now, not the past. It is all about growth and moving forward in the positive. It has no room for doubt and unbelief, and it knows and understands that all things are possible. There is absolutely nothing you cannot accomplish. The focus is in line with God's best for you, and the answer is always yes and amen! Those living in the affirmative are moving full speed ahead and picking up momentum as they continue. Women focused on the yes life view challenges differently. We do not see them as hindrances but opportunities for growth. We fully know and understand if God allowed the challenge to come, we will gain something from it to help us with our divine purpose.

JOURNAL QUESTIONS:

Where are you saying "no" and "it's not possible" to a desire in your life today and what thought process is encouraging that?

Where are you basing the decisions on moving forward in life on a past experience?

Where are you allowing a challenge to keep you from moving forward in your life and what action can you take now to do the opposite?

DIG DEEP

INTIMACY WITH SELF

Every day there is going to be an issue or hurdle that requires you to dig deep. Remember that you were created to be more than a conqueror, so celebrate those opportunities that require you to operate as such. Don't shy away from things that require a little bit more from you physically and emotionally. They just require you to dig a little deeper, so you can handle the harvest that comes as a result of the work. The road is easy for the one that is well equipped to take it. A truck will do much better on a dirt road than a ford focus. You can do this. See the challenges as opportunities for you to increase and develop your faith muscle. Your faith is crucial on this journey. It is necessary just like air and water. It is an extension of your true self. There is a certain level of discomfort that comes with change. Change requires us to do something different, and it pulls on us to get out of our comfort zone. That comfort zone is what we have created through habits. Begin to operate from that place of truth and authenticity. When we dig deep within ourselves we learn more about our strengths and weaknesses. Be mindful that while we experience these new feelings and emotions, we will also experience a new and different result. Allow yourself space to process what you are feeling. We self-sabotage all of our efforts when we don't allow ourselves space to experience the destination we've worked so hard to get to because we don't like the way it feels.

JOURNAL QUESTIONS:

What areas of your life are you afraid to confront and why?

What are some ways you can strengthen yourself to confront these areas and make changes?

PERSEVERENCE

Perseverance is the key to breakthrough!!! The opposition will come but continue to move forward and with each challenge you will become stronger, and with each accomplishment, more determined. The results are phenomenal. Accomplishment is such a wonderful feeling. When things are difficult, stay and make a decision to operate in them with a greater level of excellence. Try not to run from your opportunity for growth. If you've tried something new and it didn't work, it is ok. Pick yourself up, dust yourself off, take the lesson, and keep moving forward. Life does not end because something did not work. I am living proof that you absolutely can have the life you want. All that is necessary is a willingness to do the work and work is required. There will be discomfort at times so get comfortable with being uncomfortable. The flesh is used to doing things the old way; it does not want to accept anything new. Allow yourself to be lead by your truth, not what it feels like or looks like. With every faith step, you take there is power (ability, efficiency, might) for the next leg of the journey. Looking fear right in the eye and speaking your faith will give you a sure foot every time. Trust a faith-filled heart. When you have a plan, in the process, things will come against it to try and throw you off course. Keep moving even if you have to go slow. There is a lesson in that moment of continuing that will propel you forward. It is easier to persevere when you are intentional your goal. You know the satisfaction that comes at the expected end is far more powerful than any storm or difficulty that comes your way. Every lesson you learn will help you to gain more ground and more wisdom. You being consistent will bring you to the destination you desire, much wiser.

JOURNAL QUESTIONS:

Is there any event that has caused you to quit on pursuing your dreams? If so, what was the thought process behind your decision and is it a healthy mindset to have for the direction you want to take your life in?

A BETTER WAY

THE NEW NORMAL

The way you live your life today, your truths, your beliefs, your way of doing things, the way you think and how you react to situations have all contributed to where you are right now. You wanting something different is why you have picked up this book. The lessons I have shared with you so far are simple. When we consider them it all makes sense, and we realize that life is easy, we are the ones that have made it hard. This book is all about doing something different to get different results. We are all human, and we all miss it sometimes. The good thing is we have the power to make changes that count. Breaking Through Chaos is all about creating a new normal, where we are intimate with our truths, thinking a better way and doing it better, to receive better results.

JOURNAL QUESTIONS:

What is your "why" for change?

FROM FANTASYLAND TO REALITY

BRINGING THE DREAM DOWN TO EARTH

If you want your desires to start manifesting, you must put some action to your faith. Spiritual things go with spiritual things, and physical things go with physical things. You can hope and dream all day but, until you begin applying an action to your hopes and dreams, they will continue to be just that, hopes and dreams. The things you've desired and can now physically touch are things you felt were worth the effort. If you've been desiring it and still don't see it, the real question is why hasn't it been worth the effort?

> For a dream comes through much activity, and a fool's voice is known by his many words. Ecclesiastes 5:3 NKJV

Big vision and goal getting that leave you all over the place are fantasy land. Be clear about your vision and goals and intentional with the steps you take concerning them. We are talking about your life here. Live your life with purpose on purpose.

JOURNAL QUESTIONS:

Allow this space to be the frame work for your vision board. Begin to list the things you desire in life and things that inspire you here. A vision board is an excellent way to keep your vision before your eyes.

Have you written out in detail a plan to bring your goals to life? If not, schedule some time this month to do that and get the ball rolling.

LIVING IN THE NOW

ENJOYING LIFE TODAY

Time seems to be our biggest excuse for NOT living right now. Oh, I'll do it tomorrow, next week, next month, after the first of the year. When I have enough money. When I find the right one. You have the power to live on your terms right now, just consider all of the things you are doing today that you have not allowed time to be an excuse for. Are the desires of your heart not worth doing today? What is the real issue? One of the best decisions you can make for yourself is to live in the NOW. Not next month or if and when you accomplish something. You deserve the beauty of living today. You have already been given permission to do whatever you desire. It is in your heart today for a reason. Live in the present, because you are alive today. You are a living being today.

JOURNAL QUESTIONS:

What goal are you putting off for later?

Explain why you feel you are not worth it today.

SET BOUNDARIES, SLOW DOWN, AND ENGAGE

GETTING THE MOST OUT OF THE MOMENT

If you desire true fulfillment in your life, one of the best things you can do is to get the most out of every day. Remove the blurred lines. If it is lunch, let it be lunch. If it is family time, let it be family time. If it is work, let it be work. When your roles and the times you set for them have a purpose, you want to get the most out of that experience. Setting boundaries will keep you from being overwhelmed by having too many fires burning at one time. When we have many things going on at the same time, and our attention is spread too thin, we begin to experience mental burn out. Slow down and pay more attention to the process. Many things get lost in speed. Slowing down and engaging in the process can help you focus your energy and resources on what is needed to get the job done. Try not to be so focused on the result that you miss opportunities to celebrate accomplishments along the way. These accomplishments are the fruits of your labor and give you extra encouragement on your journey.

What are you afraid you will miss out on by doing one thing at a time and being thorough with it?

DEVELOP A HEALTHY RELATIONSHIP
WITH TIME

GET BACK IN CONTROL OF THE CLOCK

You are in control of your time; time should never control you. You decide how and where to use it. Yes, things happen beyond our control, but even at that moment, you decide how you handle that situation. You always have a choice. We spend our time how we choose too. Choose to spend your time wisely because once it is gone, you cannot get tomorrow back. If you need help, ask for it. You cannot have it all and do it all. Consider some help, maybe a personal assistant, a nanny, or a cleaning service. Doing so will take some of the stress out of your day and keep you from developing an unhealthy relationship with time, where we start obsessing over the desire for 48 hours in a day. Beware of busyness. Inspired action has a greater impact than being busy. Being busy is boring and wasteful. When we have inspired action, we get more done and receive more satisfaction from what we do. Busyness will leave you exhausted at the end of the day. When you begin to make decisions from the heart, you will no longer concern yourself with how long the process takes. You will see that these steps are all part of the big picture and necessary for the desired result.

JOURNAL QUESTIONS:

Where do you feel out of control in your daily schedule where time is concerned?

How can getting extra help allow you more time for things you enjoy and desire to pursue?

Is there anything you find yourself doing repeatedly that does not serve your purpose well and if eliminated, would allow you more time to pursue your desires?

ORGANIZING, CLEARING, AND REPLACING

MAKING ROOM FOR THE NEW

Let us take a good look at your life. How many projects do you have started, but not completed? How often are you searching for things that you use every day? How many things in your home right now are just taking up space because you have not given them a second thought in over a year? We could go on and on. My point here is that it is extremely difficult to enjoy something new when you are overwhelmed with the old. The same way you are getting rid of the old way of thinking that does not serve you well, now you need to do it in the physical. Make room in your physical life for the new things that are coming. Get your files in order, your taxes, your money. Do you have life insurance, a living will? Are there conversations you need to have with people? You will feel much lighter once you do.

JOURNAL QUESTIONS:

What needs to be organized?

What are you afraid to let go of and why?

What things do you need to get rid of that serve no purpose?

A BEAUTIFUL LIFE

MAINTAINING YOU AND FUNCTIONING EFFECTIVELY

You have a sound mind, and you know what you need to do, move on this truth today. Allow love and peace to be the foundation for your decisions as you share yourself with others from this day forward. Taking care of yourself is vital in the process of experiencing total life balance. Our lives are a direct reflection of what we believe, how we think and feel, and the decisions we make. While you are scheduling time out for work and family, be sure to take some time for you and your spiritual, mental, and physical well-being.

Schedule time to journal your journey. I love looking back over my journals and seeing my growth. Allow your journal to be your outlet at times and just a space to write it all down and figure it out. There is no judgment here; it is just an open space for you just to be whatever you need to be at that moment.

Spend time in prayer and meditation. Imagine your best possible self here. Your best self in business, in service to others, with your family. Your best self, acknowledging the presence of God in you. It is such a powerful feeling to be in at that moment and see yourself as God sees you.

Now take that power you just harvested, and take one step in being your best self. Mind you I said "in" being your best self. We spend so much time trying to be who we already are. The person you see in your meditation time is you now, your true self, and she is powerful. Take a few minutes out of your day to meditate on how you want this week to go, this month, the remainder of the year.

What you continuously meditate on you will begin to act upon, so begin to meditate daily.

Take a day where you can fellowship with your friends or have a spa day. Every woman needs some personal time for themselves. Spending time with your friends helps you to grow. You have someone just to laugh with and enjoy yourself. Then there are times when you just feel a need to relax and regroup by yourself. You are worth it and so much more.

Get your body moving with exercise and stretching, get seven to nine hours of sleep. We make much better decisions when we are well rested and make our overall health a priority.

Prepare nourishing and enjoyable meals and make your home comfortable for you and those you invite to share it with. Again, if you do not enjoy your life, why would anyone else want to share it with you.

Spend time on your hobbies. It is important to become intimate with what you like. These things are an extension of who you are. We never want to get to the point where we develop the "runaway bride" syndrome where we learn to love what everyone else loves, but have no clue as to what we enjoy. Your life will thank you, and your example will bless those you come in contact with.

Remember everything works better when it is well maintained, thus proving the importance of self-care. A well-balanced woman is more beautiful than any makeup or designer she can put on. You will find yourself operating more efficiently when you make maintaining yourself a priority.

JOURNAL QUESTIONS:

Begin to list those things that are beautiful in your life today. Use the energy you get from reminding yourself of these things and work towards adding another to the list.

CONCLUSION

I have truly enjoyed sharing my lessons with you. You will find that every area of our lives are impacted by every decision we make. Living on purpose and making decisions on purpose are vital to our success. Our purpose is woven into our lives like a beautiful thread. We should be able to see it in everything we do. We can see where we waiver on it, where we are unclear about it, even where we have completely ignored it. My prayer is that you will from this day forward absolutely never move without it. You were created with a purpose, for us to ignore it, is ignoring who we essentially are. Continue to Be!

With Love,
Liza

ABOUT THE AUTHOR

Liza Davis is a Certified Personal Development Coach, through CaPP Institute, founded by Valorie Burton, and speaker who helps women break through chaos and bring balance back to life. She is the founder of Harmony Life, a personal development and empowerment company for women. Liza stands firm in the belief that we are a spirit; we possess a soul (our mind, will, and emotions), and we live in a physical body, and believes when we align our lives with this principle, we will begin to experience total life balance and the fulfillment that comes from it.

She is no stranger to imbalance herself, in 2011 she found herself depressed and dissatisfied with her life as a result of living a chaotic lifestyle. She realized that she was not alone, as there were many women having the same experience. Liza Davis is living proof that we as women have the power to bring balance back into our lives and walk in the excellence that comes as a result of doing so.